SACAJAWEA
Wilderness Guide

by Kate Jassem
illustrated by Jan Palmer

Troll Associates

Troll Associates

Library of Congress Catalog Card Number: 78-60118
ISBN 0-89375-150-2

10 9 8 7 6 5 4 3 2

SACAJAWEA
Wilderness Guide

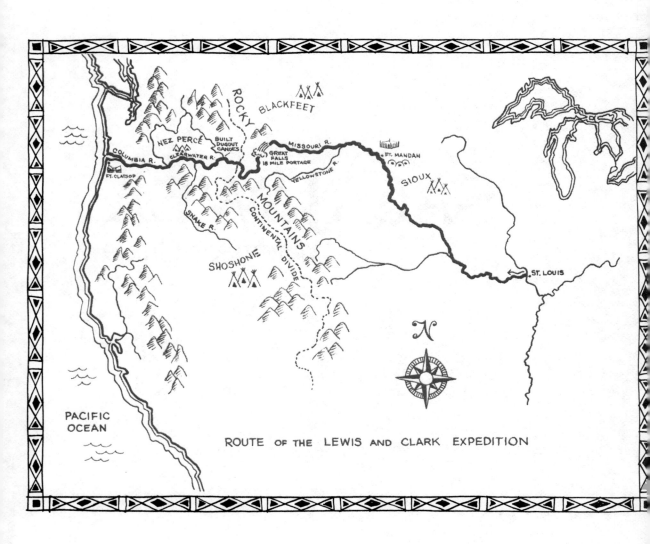

ROUTE OF THE LEWIS AND CLARK EXPEDITION

Sacajawea raced her brother Cameahwait
across the flat plain in front of the long row of
tepees.

"Faster, Arrow, faster!" she cried to her horse.

"Move, Eagle!" Cameahwait shouted. "Don't
let her catch us!"

They rode for a mile. Sometimes Sacajawea
darted ahead of her brother. Then his horse
charged into the lead.

They were both fast riders. They had the swift-
est horses because their father was Chief of the
Shoshone tribe.

5

All Shoshone braves knew how to ride. They had to move quickly to hunt the buffalo.

Once a year, the Shoshones raced down from the Rocky Mountains to hunt. Since they had no guns, they had to move fast. Down on the plains, enemy Indians had guns and wanted fine Shoshone horses.

Not every Shoshone girl could ride, and none could ride as swiftly as Sacajawea. Today she and her brother were having fun. But tomorrow, Cameahwait would ride in the hunt with the other braves. They needed the buffalo's meat and hide. Without the buffalo, they would be hungry and cold all winter.

Sacajawea and her brother rode like the wind. Suddenly, the air was filled with the crack of gunfire. Sacajawea's horse reared up, throwing her to the ground.

"Little sister!" Cameahwait cried out.

But Sacajawea did not answer.

Cameahwait was frightened. Hearing his father's loud war cry, he raced into the battle.

Soon it was done.

The Shoshone Chief fell.

Many braves died with him that day.

The rest of the Shoshones raced back to the mountains.

When Cameahwait reached the high ground, he looked down to where the camp had been. The tepees were burning. Many horses had been stolen. Smoke filled the sky.

Cameahwait felt he had lost everything. He had lost his father. He had even lost his little sister, Sacajawea. There was much sorrow.

But Sacajawea was not dead.

During the battle, she had hidden behind the rocks at the river's edge. When she saw her father fall, she cried out. Shivering with fright, she screamed again as a tall Minnetaree warrior picked her up on his stolen horse. Quickly, he rode away from the smoking Shoshone camp.

9

Now Sacajawea was a slave of the Minnetarees.

For many days they traveled fast across the
flat plains. Looking back, she could not see the
great mountains where her people lived. Her
heart was filled with sadness.

She was no longer a Shoshone princess. She
was a slave.

Her new life was strange. Her own people had been wanderers. Now, from one moon to the next, she lived in one place.

The Minnetaree houses were round mounds of earth. When winter came, she was warmer than she had been in her father's tepee. Still, she was lonely.

She was not as hungry as she had been in the mountains. With their guns, the Minnetarees could kill more buffalo. But Sacajawea often thought of her mother and sister as she sewed buffalo skins by the fire.

For three years she worked for the wives of the Minnetaree warriors. When spring came, she learned to plant corn. Working in the garden, she thought of the wild berries in the great mountains.

Then, one day, something happened that made her sure she would never see her people again.

"Sacajawea," said the Minnetaree warrior, "you have grown too old to stay with us. I have sold you to this man. You will be his wife."

Sacajawea said nothing.

"His name is Charbonneau. You will go with him."

Charbonneau was a trapper from Canada. Sacajawea did not know where his people lived. She
did not understand the words he spoke to other
white men who traveled on the river.

She hoped they would live as her people did,
hunting and trapping. But Charbonneau took her
to live near the Mandan Indians on the Missouri
River.

It was as if she had never left the Minnetarees.

That fall, Sacajawea was gathering firewood in her little boat. As she paddled toward home, she heard beating tom-toms and loud shouting.

Sacajawea was frightened. What should she do? Was this another battle?

As she came around the bend, she saw three boats. On the largest one, a bright red, white, and blue banner was waving in the wind.

Sacajawea could see many strangers. She had never seen so many white men before.

From their boats the strangers brought gifts for the Indians.

Sacajawea watched as her husband talked first to the strangers and then to the Indians. She felt proud that they needed Charbonneau to understand each other.

"Who are these men?" the Mandan Chief asked Charbonneau.

"They come from a tribe of white men." Charbonneau pointed to the east. "They come in peace."

"This is Captain William Clark." A tall red-haired man stepped forward. "He is one of their leaders."

"This is Captain Meriwether Lewis, their other leader."

"What do they want here?" asked the Mandan Chief.

"They wish to stay here for the winter. They will build a fort. When spring comes, they will travel on." Charbonneau pointed to the west.

Sacajawea felt her heart beating like tom-toms.

17

All winter, many Indians talked with the Captains. The Indians told Lewis and Clark what they knew about the land and about the tribes they would meet in the West.

Charbonneau helped them to understand the Indians' words.

One night Charbonneau told Sacajawea, "When spring comes, I will go with the Captains. They will cross the far mountains to reach the great water."

18

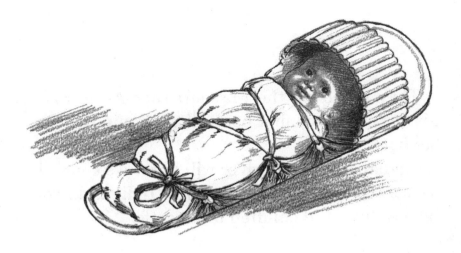

On a snowy day in February, Sacajawea's son was born. She called him Pomp.

"It is the Shoshone word for 'first-born,' " Charbonneau told the Captains.

"Shoshone?" Captain Clark asked. "She is of the Shoshone people who live in the Rocky Mountains?"

Sacajawea smiled.

"She is Shoshone," said Charbonneau.

He had told them about the Shoshone horses. The Captains knew they might need horses to cross the Rockies.

"Does she remember the language of her people? Can she help us find their camp?"

Charbonneau did not need to ask Sacajawea.

"You will come with us," he told her that night.

19

They sailed up the Missouri that April. Sacajawea sat in the first boat. Little Pomp rode on her back.

"Indians along the river will know we come in peace," Charbonneau told them. "Indians do not take women and children into battle."

Sacajawea was happy to be a sign of peace. She was even happier to be going home at last.

It was slow, hard work going up the river. And the travelers did not know that it would get harder and harder.

One day the Captains went ashore to hunt.
They left Sacajawea and Pomp with Charbonneau and another man in one of the boats on the
river.

Suddenly, a great gust of wind whipped the
boat sideways.

"Help!" Charbonneau screamed. "Help me! I
cannot swim!"

"Sit down!" Captain Lewis yelled from the
shore. "Sit down, man! You'll tip the boat over!"

"Cut the sail!" Captain Clark shouted. He was
ready to jump into the river to help, but the men
held him back.

The boat was swiftly filling with water. Charbonneau was so frightened that he was no help at all. But Sacajawea quickly grabbed many things that were starting to float away. She saved medicine, maps, and supplies that would be needed for the days ahead.

At last the boat was safely on the river bank. Captain Clark was so grateful to Sacajawea that he gave her a belt of blue beads.

For many days they traveled. After a while, they began to hear a sound like thunder. It was not thunder, but a huge waterfall!

Sacajawea was happy. She had heard her people talk of the falling water. She knew she was getting closer to her home.

"We will have to go around the falls on land," Captain Lewis decided. For weeks the men worked hard to build wagons to carry the boats on land.

Their troubles were just beginning.

It was not easy to get through the narrow canyons and up the steep, rocky hills. One day the sky seemed to open. Thunder boomed!

28

Rain rushed down, filling the narrow canyon path.

"Go up!" Captain Clark shouted. "You must climb higher up the canyon walls!"

"Oh! No!" Charbonneau screamed. He was so frightened he did not remember his wife and child.

"Higher!" Captain Clark yelled. "We must climb higher!"

"Pomp!" Sacajawea cried out. Rocks slipped under her feet.

Captain Clark grabbed Pomp. "Keep going!"

With Pomp under his arm, he helped Sacajawea and saved them both from drowning.

But their troubles were not yet over.

Along the way there were rattlesnakes and grizzly bears. Rain and hail came, and it was so cold! The path was rough and muddy. Many in the group became sick. Sacajawea almost died.

Finally, the day came when everyone felt better. Soon they were able to put the boats into the river again.

They journeyed for many long miles. Then they reached the place where the Missouri River splits into three big streams.

Captain Lewis looked at the three branches of water. Which way should he follow?

"This way," he pointed.

He named the river for his friend Thomas Jefferson, the president of the United States. Everyone prayed that they were headed in the right direction—toward the great water called the Pacific Ocean.

33

After many long days on the water, Sacajawea pointed to some round rocks on the shore. This was where she had tried to hide from the Minnetarees!

"I have been here before!" she exclaimed. She held little Pomp close to her heart. So much had passed since that day.

But where were her people?
Each day they looked for Shoshones.
"Here," Sacajawea said. "They have been here." She showed them smoking campfires along the river.
She showed them footprints of Indian feet.
But they saw no Indians.

35

"If we do not get horses, we will never make it over the mountains," Captain Lewis said. "We must find the Shoshones. I will take three men and look for them."

At last the day came.

Sacajawea heard the horses first.
Then Captain Clark heard them, too.
"My people!" she said. "My people are near."

Sacajawea walked with Captain Clark through the Shoshone camp. She looked from face to face.

She did not see her mother, her sister, or her brother. They were not here.

"Come," said Captain Clark. "We will need you to speak for us, Sacajawea."

Sadly she followed the Captains into a tall tepee and to the Shoshone Chief waiting inside.

"Cameahwait!" she cried. "My brother. I have found you."

Sacajawea threw her arms around the young Shoshone Chief.

Cameahwait could not believe what was happening!

Sacajawea's eyes filled with tears as they talked. Her mother and sister were dead. And for all these years, Cameahwait had thought she was dead, too.

Cameahwait stared at the white men and their guns. He had never seen white men before.

Sacajawea told him how Captain Clark had saved her life. He was her friend.

"Why do the white men come to the Indian's lands?" he asked.

"They need horses to cross the mountains," she replied. "They are looking for a great water, greater than any river."

"I have heard of this water," said Cameahwait. "I have never seen it. It is a long way from here."

That night Sacajawea could not sleep. Cameahwait had given the Captains twelve horses. Tomorrow they would leave.

"We need you, Sacajawea," Captain Clark had said. "Will you help us?"

How could she leave her people again?

42

"My heart is heavy," Cameahwait said, "but I know you must go."

Sacajawea could not speak.

"You will come back," Cameahwait said. "You will tell us about the great water."

Sacajawea left her people. She rode proudly on a fine Shoshone horse.

A Shoshone brave led the group into the hills.

Higher and higher they climbed. Snow and wind made each step harder. Trees blocked their way.

Sacajawea was not sure they would live to see the great water.

Cold and hungry, through narrow paths, they crossed the Rocky Mountains.

Then down, down, down they traveled. They made new boats from trees. They ate fish from the rivers.

For three long months, Sacajawea and the white men paddled down the western rivers. Indians along the shore stared at this strange group. But when they saw Sacajawea and Pomp, they let them pass.

Then one rainy November day, the long Columbia River got wider and wider.

Suddenly, there in front of them, as far as the eye could see, stretched a huge body of blue water.

"The ocean!" the men shouted. "We have reached the Pacific Ocean!"

Sacajawea remembered her brother's words. "You will come back. You will tell us about the great water."

That winter they built a fort near the Pacific
Ocean. Their red, white, and blue banner waved
in the salty air. Everyone was tired but happy.

"We have done what we set out to do!" Captain
Clark said.

Sacajawea was proud that she and her people
had helped. She looked out at the ocean. She
thought to herself, "I have seen sights I will
remember all my life. And I found my people
again. I am happy."

When spring came, Sacajawea and the others traveled back up the rivers and over the mountains.

Sadly, Sacajawea did not find Cameahwait that spring. We do not know if she ever did.

She and Charbonneau returned to the Mandan village.

Sacajawea was the first woman to cross the Rocky Mountains. With Lewis and Clark, she had helped to open the way west. She did not know that she always would be remembered for these things.

48